Find the Snake

By Cate Foley

Welcome Books

Children's Press
A Division of Grolier Publishing
New York / London / Hong Kong / Sydney
Danbury, Connecticut

Photo Credits: Cover, p. 9, 11, 21 © Joe Mc Donald/Animals Animals; p. 5, 7, 21 © Eastcott/Momatiuk/Animals Animals; p.13, 15, 21 © Maresa Pryor/Animals Animals; p.17, 19, 21 © Leonard Lee Rue III/Animals Animals
Contributing Editor: Jennifer Ceaser
Book Design: Kim Sonsky

Visit Children's Press on the Internet at:
http://publishing.grolier.com

Cataloging-in-Publication Data

Foley, Cate
    Find the Snake. / by Cate Foley.
     p. cm.—(Hide and seek)
    Includes bibliographical references (p.).
    Summary: Children look closely for snakes that can hide in their surroundings, including cotton-mouth snakes, rattlesnakes, and horned desert viper snakes.
    ISBN 0-516-23097-2 (lib. bdg.)—ISBN 0-516-23022-0 (pbk.)
    1. Snakes—Juvenile literature   2. Camouflage (Biology)—
Juvenile literature   [1.   Snakes   2.   Camouflage (Biology)]
I. Title   II.   Series
597.96—dc21   00-20923

Contents

Look closely.

Can you see green plants and mud?

A snake is there, too!

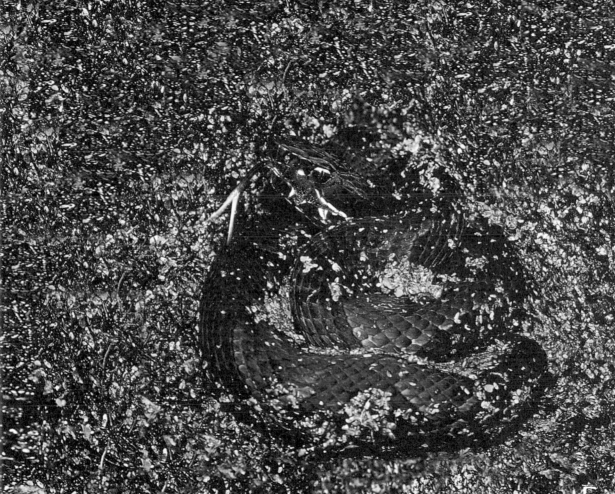

5

This is a cottonmouth snake.

This snake hides in the water.

Look closely.

Can you see **grains** of sand?

A snake is there, too!

This is a **horned** desert viper snake.

This snake hides in the sand.

11

Look closely.

Can you see the **branches**?

A snake is there, too!

This is a tree boa snake.

This snake curls around a branch to hide.

15

Look closely.

Can you see leaves and sticks?

A snake is there, too!

17

This is a rattlesnake.

This snake hides on the ground.

19

Which snake do you like the best?

21

New Words

branches (**branch**-ez) parts of a tree that grow out from the trunk

grains (**graynz**) tiny bits of sand

horned (**hornd**) something with horns, or points, on its head

To Find Out More

Books
Animal Hide-And-Seek
by Teddy Slater and Donna Braginetz Bantam
Doubleday Dell Books for Young Readers

Outside and Inside Snakes
by Sandra Markle
Simon & Schuster Children's

Web Site
The Reptile House
http://www.lazoo.org/reptiles.htm
Read about the reptiles in the Los Angeles Zoo.
Learn about different kinds of snakes.

23

Index

branches, 12, 14

cottonmouth, 6

grains, 8

horned desert
viper, 10

leaves, 16

mud, 4

rattlesnake, 18

sand, 8, 10

sticks, 16

tree boa, 14

About the Author
Cate Foley writes and edits books for children. She lives in New Jersey with her husband and son.

Reading Consultants

Kris Flynn, Coordinator, Small School District Literacy, The San Diego County Office of Education

Shelly Forys, Certified Reading Recovery Specialist, W.J. Sahnow Elementary School, Waterloo, IL

Peggy McNamara, Professor, Bank Street College of Education, Reading and Literacy Program